The Goalie Coach Handbook

Brian Bush
San Diego, California, USA

The Goalie Coach Handbook

© 2010 by Club 39 Publishing
All rights reserved.

ISBN 9781453850930

Printed in the United States of America.

Preface

Before we get started, I would like to take a minute to discuss gender in goaltending. This book is intended to help male and female goaltenders. Use of the male pronoun is not in any way meant to be a slight against female goalies. It was done this way for ease and consistency of typing for a first time author.

The Goalie Coach Handbook

Acknowledgements

Like any other book this one could not be written without the help and inspiration of others. I would like to thank Chris Webb for first getting me involved in hockey. Jeremy Dries for being with me every step of the way. Thank you to Paul Chapey for organizing an instructional league for us to learn and play in. Jason Carver for insisting I write a book. James Haug for always being a great friend. My mom and dad for always supporting me and mom for editing this book. And finally to my love Jennifer Nakayama for inspiring me to step outside of my comfort level and excel to greatness.

Table of Contents

Preface i
Acknowledgements iii
Welcome 1
Choosing a Goalie 4
   Beginning Goalies 4
   Experienced Goalies 6
Equipment 9
   Skates 11
   Leg Pads 12
   Goalie Pants 13
   Chest Protector 14
   Catcher & Blocker 15
   Goalie Mask 15
   Goalie Stick 16
Goaltending Styles 18
   Stand-Up 18
   Butterfly 19
   Hybrid 21
Goalie Stances 23
Skating 27
Goalie Mobility 32
Playing Angles 36
Goalie Flexibility 46
Save Techniques 50
   Stick Saves 51
   Poke Check 53
   Kick Saves 54
   Stacking the Pads 56

- Glove & Blocker Saves 56
- Upper Body Saves 58
- Playing the Puck 61
- Seeing the Puck 67
- Fear of the Puck 72
- Focus 76
- Pulling Your Goalie 81
- Confidence 86
- Mental Toughness 92
- The Extra Attacker 98
- Situational Goaltending 102
  - Breakaways 102
  - 2 on 0's and 3 on 0's 103
  - 1 on 1's and 1 on 2's 104
  - 2 on 1's 104
  - 3 on 1's 105
  - Rebounds 105
  - Wraparounds 106
  - In-zone face-offs 107
  - Deflections 108
  - Communication 108
- Glossary 110

1

Welcome

The fact is most hockey coaches have never played goalie. This in and of itself is not a bad thing, but it does leave goaltenders without clear direction. This is your resource to fill that knowledge gap.

Welcome to *The Goalie Coach Handbook*. This book is designed to help coaches and parents give clear direction to beginning goaltenders. For too long coaches' advice to goalies consisted of "go stop the puck." This book aims to change all of that.

Welcome

The Goalie Coach Handbook will cover a wide variety of topics some coaches did not even know existed in goaltending. It contains information to provide a strong foundation for a goaltender on which to build his game.

Even though this book is designed for beginning goaltenders, there is still a lot of helpful information to help even the most advanced goaltenders take their games to the next level.

You should read the book straight through, as you might find some aspects of goaltending are more important than you might have thought. After that, the content in this book is designed for quick access so you can refer to information before, during, and after practice.

With *The Goalie Coach Handbook*, the most inexperienced coaches will be able to consistently develop practice plans that will benefit their whole team. No more having your goalies stand in the net with nothing to do while the skaters practice skating drills.

Better knowledge equals better goalies. You hold in your hand the knowledge to make any goalie you coach better without ever having to have a puck shot at you. You now have the great advantage that coaches look for. I would tell you good luck; but with this book, you won't need it.

2

Choosing a Goalie

Beginning Goalies

When forming a youth hockey team, there is one position almost every young player wants to play: goalie. You will most likely have no shortage of volunteers your first couple weeks of the season as kids flock towards the cool-looking equipment and the feeling of security the oversized pads provide.

It is very important, however, as a coach or parent to understand that just because a child wants to play goal early on that he won't change his mind the first time someone shoots a puck at him. That is why it is important to allow all of the interested kids on the team that want to try out being the goalie the opportunity.

The Goalie Coach Handbook

(Note to parents: Goalie equipment can be very costly. It is very important to your bank account that your child is serious about goaltending before you make the investment. It is best to let them try it out if possible.)

There is a longstanding myth that in youth hockey you can just put the worst skater on the team in goal and everything will be fine. This is the worst possible thing you can do for two reasons.

1. Goaltending has become an incredibly athletic position. Putting a player that can't move in net will dramatically hinder your team's ability to keep the other team from outscoring you.

2. The poor skater you put in goal will never have the opportunity to learn to be a good skater.

When dealing with young goalies, choosing one to start your games is more about which of your players is willing to play goal. If you don't have any volunteers, then I highly recommend that you cycle through all of your players. Usually one of them will find that they enjoy it, and you will have found your new goalie. If none of them are interested, then continue the cycle.

This will help with the team building aspect of coaching. Since all of the team is expected to take their turn in goal, you will encounter less complaining. Don't be afraid to put your best offensive player in goal. If they really like it and no one else does, it is worth the tradeoff. You will come to find that teaching players that are less skilled offensively to score goals is easier than teaching a young child not to be afraid of the puck.

Experienced Goalies

Choosing an experienced goalie is a little bit trickier. This book assumes that if you are reading this section, you are dealing with goalies that have a few seasons under their belts and that you won't need to deal with fear of the puck or searching for someone on your team that is willing to play goal.

There are two different times you will have to choose a goalie for your team at this level.

1. You are drafting a team for a house league or you are drafting a goalie for a professional team.

2. You have two or more goalies on your team and you need to decide who should be your starter for any given game.

In each of the above cases, you should pretty much be looking for the same types of signs when choosing a starting goalie. The only real difference is: When you are trying to decide which goalie to start individual games, you need to watch a lot more closely. Here is a quick summery of what to look for when choosing a goalie.

Vision: Can the goalie see the puck?

You might think this is a foolish question when you can clearly see the goalie is moving with the puck and making saves, but let me explain what I mean by seeing the puck. A goalie can see the puck as it moves around the rink; but when the puck is shot, they lose it off the blade and drop into the Butterfly to take away the bottom of the net. When this happens, the goalie is not really seeing the puck but reacting to events around the rink. I will talk more about how you can tell if a goalie is seeing the puck in a later chapter.

Mobility: How well does the goalie move around the crease?

Choosing A Goalie

This is the reason that you don't put the worst skater on the team in goal. A goalie's mobility is very, very important. You'll need to look at your goalie's ability to move.

Angles: How well does the goalie play his angles?

Angles are mostly tied to mobility. A goalie that can play angles well can be less talented in other areas and still be a much better goalie.

Confidence: How confident does the goalie look?

Confidence is the most important trait in good goaltenders. You want a goalie that wants the puck shot at them not one that is afraid of it.

Finding a good goalie is not as much a lottery when you know what to look for. The good news is: With this book, you will not only be able to identify these traits in goalies, you will be able to engrain them. So let's get started.

3

Equipment

Goalie equipment is one of the key reasons kids decide they want to play goal. Let's face it: Goalie equipment is just cool. The large pads make the goalies feel like they are indestructible. The goalie mask lets goalies remain somewhat anonymous while at the same time expressing an artistic side of themselves not often seen off the rink.

Sometimes goalies or their parents will want to make sure they are well protected -- beyond well protected, actually. They will want to get the biggest pads they can find that will still fit. Some goalies actually believe that wearing leg pads that are too long will help them close their five-holes and make them tougher to score on.

Equipment

For goalies, wearing oversized equipment is a bad idea. It might provide a false sense of security. They believe that more padding will help to keep them safer. This is not really the case at all. Goalie equipment is designed to fit goalies properly so that it can provide maximum protection as well as maximum mobility.

When goalies wear pads that are oversized, they limit their mobility. This seriously hinders their ability to protect themselves. There will always be holes in the goalies' equipment that a puck can squeak through and cause pain. If a goaltender's mobility is limited, then he can't move quickly enough to close those holes in the armor.

Along with the injury risk, goaltenders that have hindered their mobility will allow more goals. The belief that longer pads equal more saves is the primary culprit of these goals. Longer pads seem like a great idea. With longer pads, goalies don't have to get their knees together when they Butterfly. They can just drop, and the pads will cover the five-hole.

This is all good in theory, but in actual game situations it doesn't work out so smoothly. But before we get to that, let's talk about skates.

Skates

Goalie skates are different from regular hockey skates. For ice they have a long, flat blade instead of the shorter more rounded blades of the skaters. For roller hockey goalies, skates have shorter frames with five small wheels instead of the four larger ones on the skaters'. The reason: It provides more stability and quicker side-to-side movements for goaltenders. Skaters' skates are built for speed and quick turns at speed.

In addition to the difference in the blades and frames on goalie skates, the boot is generally cut lower at the ankle line than skater skates. This allows for more flexibility through the ankles.

The other major difference in goalie skates and skater skates is goalie skates have a hard plastic casing. This provides additional protection for the goalie's feet as pucks can find their way past leg pads and into more sensitive instep areas.

Goalie skates are sized much like regular shoes. It is a good idea when trying on skates to aim for having them a little bit tight. The reason: The padding that goes into skates these days is designed to mold to your feet. So if the skates are loose when you buy them, they will get looser as they are worn.

Equipment

Leg Pads

Now that we have talked about goalie skates, let's move on to the leg pads. As I said before, having oversized leg pads especially in length can hurt a goalie more than it can help.

Longer leg pads do weigh more than shorter ones, but that is not the primary reason for allowing more goals. The reason longer leg pads cause goalies to allow more goals is that it hinders the goalie's ability to get his legs completely closed in the Butterfly. This is the opposite of what most people think. If you try and move your legs together to Butterfly, the longer your pads are the farther apart you will have to have your feet. If you don't have your feet far enough apart, the pads will hit each other on the way down and get hung up, leaving a gap between the legs and the five-hole open.

To combat this problem, some goalies will make the straps on the upper thigh tighter. This will force the pads to bend in areas that they are designed to bend. This, of course, decreases mobility and is counterproductive. A set of goalie leg pads should be strapped tight from the skates to the knee. Around the knee and to the top of the pad, they should be loose allowing for a greater range of motion.

In order to properly size a set of leg pads as well as order them online, you will need to know your goalie's skate size. Measure your goalie's leg from the inside middle of the ankle bone to the front center of the knee cap with the leg slightly bent, and then add six to seven inches to that number for the rise of the pad up the thigh. This will provide maximum protection and maximum mobility.

There is one other thing a goalie needs to consider when purchasing leg pads: There is the option of the thigh guards. Thigh guards either come stitched into the leg pads or the goalie's pants. Thigh guards protect the sensitive area of the thigh between leg pad and goalie pants. You need to make sure that one piece of equipment or the other has this important protection.

Goalie Pants

Moving on to the next piece of equipment: Goalie pants are very similar to regular ice hockey skater's pants on the outside. On the inside, however, they are different. They contain much more padding, particularly in the inside of the thigh area. The other difference as mentioned above is that some pairs of goalie pants will have thigh guards. Do not get thigh guards in both goalie pants and leg pads. They will not provide more protection. In fact, you will need to cut them out of either the leg pads or goalie pants for them to work properly. Other than the extra padding, there is no trick to buying goalie pants. Having your goalie's waist size should be all that you need.

Chest Protector

Next on the list for goalie equipment is the chest protector. The chest protector is actually more than just a chest protector. It covers the goalie's arms, too. When wearing the chest protector, it should be worn tight around the torso so that it cannot shift during the course of the game. It should also be tight around the arms but not so tight that it limits range of motion.

To measure your goalie for proper fit for a chest protector, you need to measure in inches from under the armpits around the chest. If you can try it on before you buy, make sure that it covers all areas of the upper body.

Catcher & Blocker

Next up is the catcher and the blocker. The catching glove is most commonly just referred to as "the glove" and resembles a baseball glove. It has a deep pocket for catching pucks, a large wrist guard to protect the underside of the wrist, and padding on the backside of the hand to protect against sticks trying to pry loose a covered puck.

The blocker is a large padded guard that protects the back side of the hand and forearm that holds the stick. It is used most effectively to steer shots into the corner away from the front of the net.

The glove and blocker are the same in regard to fitting. Sizes are based on age, and the glove and blocker should fit loosely. There should be enough room in the cuffs for the arms of the chest protector to slide into.

Goalie Mask

Next up is the goalie mask. The goalie mask should fit snuggly on a goaltender's head so that it does not move around as the goaltender looks from side to side. The goalie mask must be HECC approved for safety reasons. There are two different types of cages for a goalie mask, standard and cat's eye.

Equipment

Youth goalies are required to wear standard. To ensure proper fit for a goalie mask, you should measure the circumference of your goalie's head at the forehead.

Most goalie masks have a throat drop feature that helps protect the throat from shots. For added protection, goalies can get a throat protector, which come in two styles. The first one hangs down from the goalie masks and is usually tied on with skate laces. This version is a harder plastic and works well to keep pucks away from the throat completely. The second version is padding that is strapped around the throat. This also works well, but a hard enough shot can still cause pain. If you or the goalie is overly worried about pucks hitting his throat, it is possible to wear both types of protection.

Goalie Stick

Last but not least, we come to the goalie stick. The goalie stick is purely a matter of preference for the goaltender. There is actually no standard method of measurement for them. Contrary to popular belief, it doesn't directly correlate to the goalie's height. The best advice I can give you is to visit a retailer where the goalie can try holding a few and get what feels best to him.

For a list of the best online retailers of all the types of goalie equipment in this chapter, visit our website at www.TheGoalieCoach.com.

4

Goaltending Styles

In hockey today there are three widely recognized goaltending styles.

1. Stand-Up.
2. Butterfly.
3. Hybrid.

Here is a brief history and description of the styles of goaltending.

Stand-Up

The style of Stand-Up is the most basic and the oldest style of goaltending. Stand-Up goalies are all but extinct these days. All of the early NHL greats were your classic Stand-Up goaltenders. Back in the early 1900's, they really had no choice. Goalies were penalized for dropping to their knees. That was also an era when teams only had one goalie, and they had to serve their own penalties. So you can see how short-handed your team would be if the goalie took a penalty.

Stand-Up goaltending is just like it sounds. The goalie stays on his feet to stop all of the shots. The only time a goalie would drop to his knees is if the puck was right at his feet. While Stand-Up is almost extinct at higher levels of play, many beginning goalies still use this basic style.

The reason for this is that beginner goalies usually have not developed the flexibility or the muscle coordination to quickly drop and immediately get back up for another shot. The other benefit to the Stand-Up style for beginners is that they can keep their eyes on the same plane at all times so that they can track the puck easier and make the save.

Butterfly

The style of Butterfly has its roots in the mid-1950's with Glenn Hall, but it didn't become a NHL mainstay until Patrick Roy of the Montreal Canadiens began

Goaltending Styles

dominating the league with it in the late 1980's. Now almost all of the goalies in the NHL play the Butterfly style of goaltending.

There is some dispute as to where the name Butterfly came from, but it is hard to argue the effectiveness of this style. The Butterfly is where goalies drop to their knees on low shots kicking their legs out towards both posts in  an inverted V. This allows goalies to take away the low corners of the net. Provided they keep their stick covering the five-hole between their legs, they can cover the whole bottom of the net.

Some goalies will cheat with this style and drop on every shot. They do this to hide the fact that they are not seeing the puck come off the stick when the puck is shot. The odds of the shot being low are greater so the puck will hit them more if they can cover the bottom of the net.

You might be wondering what is wrong with that. You are saying "As a coach I want the puck to hit my goalie". The problem is when a puck just hits the goalie without the goalie knowing it; they give up big juicy rebounds. If you don't have a defense that is always there to clear the puck, you give up a lot of goals.

For a goalie to be good at the Butterfly style, they need to have good flexibility, core strength, and quick hands to get to the pucks that are shot high.

Hybrid

There are two versions of the Hybrid style of goaltending. Hybrid goaltending is a mix between the Stand-Up style and the Butterfly style.

The first Hybrid style made its appearance in the 1940's and grew to popularity in the 1950's. Goalies played mostly Stand-Up style, but they started to go down more over time to stop shots. They would not go into a Butterfly, but they did spend more time on their knees than in any other area previously.

The second Hybrid style is making its debut right now. More and more goalies have begun to stay on their feet more and are not dropping so much. Goaltenders like Martian Brodeur of the New Jersey Devils have used this style to become some of the greatest NHL goaltenders of all time.

Goaltending Styles

You might be wondering which style I feel is best. I believe it is a personal decision for a goalie. When they are beginning at a young age, I would definitely recommend Stand-Up style to teach them to see the puck properly. This will build a great foundation for them to move to a Butterfly or Hybrid style in the future.

That being said, it is up to the goalie to know when it is time to choose a style and which style to choose. They may start as a Stand-Up goalie but quickly move to a Butterfly or Hybrid style, or they may be a Stand-Up goalie for life.

The best way for a goalie to find his style is to get comfortable in his stance and do whatever he can to stop the puck. When it comes to goalies' styles, whatever works for them works. There is no such thing as an ugly save. Many goalies will shift styles throughout their goaltending careers, and many will develop new tactics that will be copied by others.

As a coach you should not get too hung up on the style your goaltender uses. Tinkering with their style can cause some major problems in their game. It is, however, important for you to have knowledge of the styles so you can properly address other areas of concern for them; but it is important to remember it is a personal choice for your goalie.

Goalie Stances

A goaltender's stance is the foundation of his game. The goalie stance can make or break a goaltender. It is usually the reason they play well or poorly. Goalies can lose their stance even at the NHL level. When this happens, you will see a marked drop-off in their ability to make saves.

A goalie's stance will vary by the individual. The stance needs to be comfortable enough that a goalie can stand in his stance for the entire game if necessary and not tire out. Oftentimes a goalie's stance will come about based on his particular style of play. This is why it is important that goalies be able to find their own stance.

Goalie Stances

As important as individual style is to a goaltender's stance, it is important to remember that there are some basic principles to keep in mind that will make stopping the puck much easier. Here are three things for your goalies to keep in mind while finding their stances.

1. Keep your weight centered on the balls of your feet. This will keep you from being caught flat-footed and will increase your mobility. (Mobility is very important to a

goaltender and will be discussed at length in chapter #7.)

2. Bend your knees so that they are in line with the balls of your feet. This provides solid balance and allows you to be mobile and ready for low shots.

3. Line your shoulders up slightly forward of your knees and the balls of your feet. This helps keep your weight forward so that you can aggressively move to the puck. When goalies go down to the Butterfly position (see chapter # 6 on Styles) to make a save, they leave the top portion of the net open. Goalies that don't have their shoulders slightly ahead of their knees and feet have a tendency to become lazy and rock back onto their bottoms pulling their shoulders down and opening up more of the high part of the net.

In order to help young and beginning goalies find their stances, it is important to instruct them on the above three steps. Then have them get into a stance that they feel comfortable in with no equipment on. Let them find their own comfort level where they feel like they can stand for awhile without becoming tired.

Goalie Stances

After they find a stance they feel comfortable in, have them try it with skates and pads on. Although I highly recommend having your goalies work on skating drills with the rest of the team, working on their stances during what would normally be dead time for goalies in practice is also a suitable use of time. Goalies should never be idle during practice when the rest of the team is working on drills. They should be treated as any other member of the team.

Once your goalie feels comfortable with his stance, you can move on to whichever style your goalie is comfortable playing. Don't be worried if you notice a shift in your goalie's stance as he discovers his personal style of goaltending. Many goalies will tweak their stance to match their particular style. This is a trial-and-error learning experience for all goalies at all levels. If this results in a sharp drop-off in play, you can talk to them about it. It might just be some minor growing pains in their overall development.

6

Skating

I know what you are thinking. You're thinking: Why is there a chapter about skating in a book about goaltending? The reason is because skating is a tremendously important aspect of goaltending.

Most people, including coaches, think that it is perfectly acceptable to put the kid that can't skate in goal. This couldn't be further from the truth. Today's goaltenders need not only to be good athletes, but they need to be good skaters. Here is a scenario using current NHL stars that will explain why.

Skating

Imagine the Pittsburgh Penguins are playing the New Jersey Devils. The score late in the game is the Devils three, the Penguins two. All of a sudden the Devils have an uncharacteristic lapse in defense and turn the puck over to Sidney Crosby along the boards at the red line. Crosby now has a clear breakaway on Devils goalie Martin Brodeur.

The first thing that Brodeur does after seeing the turnover is skate out of the bottom of the face-off circles to help cut down the angle. This makes it so that Crosby cannot take a quick shot from distance and easily beat him.

Crosby looks up and sees that by skating out, Brodeur has cut down the angle so he decides to try to get in close to deke him instead. Crosby moves in from Brodeur's left. He fakes to the short side and tries to skate around to Brodeur's right.

Because Brodeur is a great skater he is able to move back to his net at the same pace that Crosby is moving towards the net. When Crosby dekes to Brodeur's left, he is able to stay on his feet and not fall for the move.

If Brodeur were a bad skater, he would most likely drop to his knees in the Butterfly position at this point. This would make it very easy for Crosby to go around to his right.

Crosby continues around to Brodeur's right and tries to fully extend his stick to reach around Brodeur and tuck the puck home, but Brodeur's skating ability allows him to follow Crosby's move to Brodeur's right and extend his right skate to kick the puck away when Crosby tries to tuck it home.

Not only does Brodeur's skating ability allow for him to make the save and preserve the lead for his team, he was also able to kick the rebound from the dangerous position in front of the net.

This scenario illustrates that skating is important to a goaltender even if the coaches or even the goalies themselves do not realize it. It also illustrates the little known fact that good goalies can be considered better skaters than position players.

Think about the above scenario again. Think about what it would look like for Sidney Crosby (one of the best skaters in the game) to have a breakaway from the center red line. Think of the speed he would be bearing down on Brodeur with, how well he would fake to the left and skate across to the right.

Skating

Now realize that as Brodeur mirrored Crosby's movements to make the save, he skated just as well as Crosby. The reason he is a better skater is that Brodeur did it backwards and sideways, the whole time keeping his angle between the net behind him that he cannot see and the puck being dangled in front of him at the end of a five-foot-long stick.

This is what can and will happen if you have a goalie that is a great skater. If your goalie is a good skater, they can probably make the save described above, but they will not be able to clear the rebound into the corner. This can be enough; but eventually not clearing the rebound will result in goals being scored. If your goalie is a poor skater, then they wouldn't come out to cut down the angle, and the shooter will just shoot the puck past them from a distance: if they want to show off, they will easily skate around your goalie and score.

There is no downside to having a good skater in goal. To achieve this, the goalies on your team should be involved in all skating drills that do not involve shots on a goalie at the end. Have your goalies run the same stick handling drills you have the rest of your team run, make them participate in Herbie's or suicides. And most importantly have them participate in all backward skating drills.

The Goalie Coach Handbook

Practice tip: Have your team skate warm-up laps at the beginning of practice, skaters skating forward and goalies skating backward. Blow your whistle and have your skaters switch to backwards and your goalies skate to forward until you blow the whistle again. Repeat this several times at random intervals.

I can go on and on about how important skating is to goaltenders, but I am hoping that you are starting to see that for yourself. Remember: There is no reason for a goalie to be standing around during practice. This will build a stronger bond between your team if goalies aren't given drills off because it's a skating drill and the goalies don't think they should have to do it. **All players, all drills, every practice**. If you remember this, your goalie will be stronger, your team will be stronger, and the wins will keep on piling up.

7

Goalie Mobility

Just like skating, mobility for a goaltender is a very underrated yet very important part of the game. Mobility is what turns good goalies into great goalies.

The roots of mobility are in skating. A goalie that can't skate can't be mobile. Fortunately for you coaches out there, by applying the lesson from the last chapter and having your goalie skate in all drills with the team you are that much closer to having a mobile goaltender.

You might be wondering what the difference in skating and mobility really is. In the case of goalies, we will classify skating as moving forward to come out and cut down the angles on breakaways, staying with the shooter by following him/her across the net on dekes, coming out of the net to play loose pucks and so on and so forth.

Mobility has everything that skating has plus it has a lot to do with a goalie's ability to make small and subtle changes in position to ensure that the goalie is always cutting down the angle and providing the least amount of open net for the shooter.

At this point a lot of you coaches are probably thinking that I am overstating the importance of a goalie being able to skate and be mobile. A lot of you are thinking: I coach 5-year-olds. I'm lucky if the kid can even move in those pads. Here are the two best reasons for you to instill strong skating habits in your goalies.

1. The other coaches in the league will not be doing this. So by the second half of the season, you will have the only 5-year-old goalie in the league that can easily move to both sides of the net to make saves.

2. This is by far the most important reason. As a youth hockey coach, you are responsible not just to win the games you play that season, but to provide a solid foundation for the kids that play for you to move to the next

Goalie Mobility

level. Think of how proud you will be when you start seeing the kids you built the foundation for excel at the next level.

The small subtle changes I spoke of earlier help a goalie to cut down the angles that a shooter has to put the puck past the goalie. (The importance of cutting down angles will be dealt with in depth in a later chapter.) These subtle changes involve the goalie being able to make quick corrections with his feet to slide over inches at a time without having to turn his body away from the puck.

A goalie that has good mobility will have no problem with opposing defensemen that pass the puck back and forth at the blue line before taking shots. Goalies with good mobility will often deter the opposing team from shooting the puck by always being directly in front of them when they look up to take a shot. Goalies with poor mobility will find themselves out of position on simple passes that don't span much more than a couple of feet.

To improve on your goalie's mobility, you need to have your goalie partake in all skating drills that do not naturally end up with a shot on goal. I can't stress enough that it is not enough to force a shot in at the end of a skating drill because you think that the more shots a goaltender sees the better they will get. You need to build a strong foundation for a goalie to advance at a quicker pace and not get discouraged.

Practice tip: *Have your goalie move slowly across the arch of the crease while never turning his body sideways. Once he makes it to the end, have him move back to the far post as fast as he can, hugging the post. Then have him quickly move to the opposite post, again hugging the post and slowly move back across the top of the crease just like he did in the beginning of this drill. Have him move across the top of the crease five times in each direction. This can be done by goalies while coaches are explaining and setting up drills designed for shooters to take shots at the goalies.*

Since most of the rewards for mobility pay off in the proper playing of angles, we should move on to the angles chapter of the book. If you have any questions or thoughts on mobility, you can visit the website at www.TheGoalieCoach.com.

Playing Angles

In the previous chapters, we discussed the importance of skating and mobility for a goalie. In this chapter about angles, you will see how those two concepts blend together to make your beginning goalie a great one.

Angles are the single most important aspects of a goalie's game. They will make the most difference in saves and goals, wins and losses. In order to properly play angles, however, a goalie needs to be mobile on his skates, which is why the preceding chapter discusses skating and mobility first.

To properly teach goalies to play their angles correctly, it will help if you have an understanding of why angles are so important.

The Goalie Coach Handbook

A regulation hockey net is 6 feet wide by 4 feet tall. A regulation hockey puck is 1 inch tall and 3 inches round. I point this out for you to realize that a regulation hockey net consists of 24 square feet of area for a hockey puck that is 3 inches in size to go into. That means that it takes 1152 regulation hockey pucks to fill the opening in one regulation hockey net.

When thought about like this, you might start to see how hard goaltending really is. Having this information at your disposal might make you think you need to put the biggest goalie you can find in the net. I caution you on this for two reasons.

Playing Angles

1. You will not ever find a goalie large enough to take up the whole net. There are too many holes for a puck to find its way through.

2. A small goalie that can play his angles and move quickly to make the save is a much better option than a large goalie that takes up more net, but stands there and can't move.

A small goalie that can skate well and keep his angles can make a talented opposing team not even shoot the puck. You might not believe it, but I have seen it and been a part of it many times.

Every time the opposing team's players look up from the puck to shoot they see the goalie there with no open holes. In this case, they will pass again and again to try and find someone with a shot when the goalie is off his angle. If your goalie skates well and is mobile, then the chances of your goalie being off of his angle are greatly reduced. This means more passes for the opposing team and more chances your defense will break up the play without even a single shot taken on your goalie.

The Goalie Coach Handbook

Some of you are thinking: What if I get a big goalie and teach them to play angles? That would be the best option for my team. In that case you are right; but as illustrated above, you will need to go back to the previous chapters and make sure that you and your goalie work very hard on skating and mobility. You will also want to pay close attention to the upcoming chapter on flexibility, because when a goalie plays his angles well, the best way to score on him is with a cross-ice pass.

I hope by this point I have convinced you how important coaching your goalie to play his angles well is, but just in case here is one more benefit. I realize about 90% of you reading this book are youth coaches and parents. And if you are not reading this book to help your child, then you are a youth coach with access to only one goalie. The fact of the matter is that all goalies will have slumps. In fact all players in all sports will have slumps. The fastest and sometimes only way out of a slump is to work hard on your fundamentals. For goalies skating, mobility, and angles are the fundamentals that will get them through slumps faster. Taking away angles from the shooter will allow them to face fewer shots. When shots do come, they will be shot right into them. This will help with the all important confidence we will discuss in a later chapter.

Playing Angles

Enough about why it is important for goalies of any age and size to learn how to play their angles. Let us move on to how to coach them to play their angles.

There are several methods to coaching goalies in angle play, and all of them will work. You must remember that goalies as people all learn things in different ways and at different speeds. Run your goalie through a variety of methods and look for that light going on at a moment of understanding. If that doesn't happen, then it is up to you to notice which drills and exercises are helping your goalie to understand the concept of angles faster.

The exercises listed below are listed in a specific order to help the coaches' and goalies' understanding of angles first and, secondly, to help the goalies with visual aids so they can grasp the idea of angles quicker.

<u>It is very important for goalies and their coaches to understand that the **angles are from the puck** itself not the shooter.</u>

The first exercise for teaching angles is much easier now with digital cameras and camera phones. It is called Picture Time.

The Goalie Coach Handbook

1. You stand in the middle of the face-off dots. Have your goalie stand in the middle of his net with the back of his skates touching the goal line. Have him get into his stance. Take a picture.

2. Stay where you are and have the goalie move out to the top of the crease, get into his stance, and take a picture.

3. Stay where you are and have the goalie move out two feet above the top of the crease, get into his stance, and take a picture.

Once this is done, you and the goalie should review the pictures that you took. You will notice in the first picture that there are all kinds of open net areas for the opposing shooter to try and score. The second picture should show a drastic improvement with a lot less net available to the shooter. The third picture should have no net available to the shooter and should be an example of overplaying your angles. Overplaying your angles should only be done in extreme circumstances and only if your goalie is a good enough skater to get back in proper position to not allow a goal. Some of these extreme circumstances -- breakaways, 2-on-1's -- will be discussed in chapter #19, *Situational Goaltending*

Playing Angles

The second exercise for helping goaltenders learn how to find their angles is called The Rope Trick.

The Rope Trick is done by getting two lengths of rope. A 100-foot length of nylon rope cut in half should be enough.

1. Place a puck on the rink somewhere in the defensive zone. (Early on it is best to place it towards the middle of the rink, but you can use different areas for more advanced angles.)

2. Tie a length of rope to each of the posts.

3. Extend the ropes out to the puck that you placed earlier forming a triangle from each post to the puck.

4. Have your goalie stand in the net with his skates on the goal line.

5. Have the goalie get into his goalie stance.

6. Now have your goalie move out toward the puck cutting down the angle. He will know he is at the right position to cut down the angle when his skates touch each of the ropes while he is in his stance.

This exercise can be done by moving the puck to different areas inside the defensive zone. Work on more and more extreme angles as the goalies get more comfortable

Helpful hint: *During these exercises, it is helpful to encourage your goalie to look for landmarks on the rink in relation to his position. These landmarks can be anything that helps a goalie to know where he is without having to look back at the net. (Marks or advertisements on the board, graphics on the rink, etc...)*

The third exercise is called Puck Placement.

1. The coach or goalie places a puck on the goal line in the center of the net.

2. The goalie gets into his goalie stance with a second puck in his catching glove.

3. A shooter (usually a coach or assistant) skates around the defensive zone with a third puck while the goalie follows his movements attempting to cut down the angle.

4. After about 20 to 30 seconds, the shooter stops.

Playing Angles

5. The goalie then takes the puck from his catching glove and places it on the rink at the center of his body (usually right between his legs).

6. The goalie then skates out to the shooter's position and looks back at the net.

7. Looking back at the net, the shooter's puck, the goalie's puck, and the puck on the goal line should form a straight line.

8. After looking at the line of pucks, you can have the shooter stand over the goalie's puck in a goalie stance to show the goalie how much space the shooter has to shoot at. This will help emphasize the point of the exercise and drive the lesson home.

By repeating these exercises as well as having your goalies participate in skating drills with the rest of the team, your goalies should be able to quickly master their angles and become much more effective goaltenders.

Important note: *Sometimes when a goalie slumps, it is because he is off of his angles. It is a good idea to* *revisit these exercises from time to time to help avoid this.*

There are many more drills that deal with angles available in *The Goalie Coach Drill Book*. Visit www.TheGoalieCoach.com to upload video for personal review and visit the goaltenders and coaches forums.

Goalie Flexibility

For goalies, flexibility is key to the position; not just because the more flexible a goalie is the more saves they can make, but it serves to greatly reduce the risk of injury. The position of goaltender is prone to suffer soft-tissue injuries consisting mostly of pulled muscles, ligament tears, and strains.

These types of injuries are much worse than broken bones for an athlete. Broken bones can be seen on x-rays, they can be casted and immobilized for repair, and they can be x-rayed again to see that they are fixed. Soft-tissue damage has none of those benefits. Soft-tissue damage can be very painful, does not show up on x-ray, and can be reinjured very easily if rushed back into playing.

The good news about soft-tissue injuries is that they are easily avoided. Pucks will not cause them, anything more than a bruise normally. Other than bruises, soft-tissue injuries can be avoided by having a proper stretching routine to increase flexibility, not just for your goaltenders but for all of your other players as well.

It was once believed that doing some deep stretching before practice or playing a game was the best way to avoid injury and increase flexibility. According to studies cited at www.exrx.net it turns out that deep stretching before practices and games can actually increase a player's chance of soft-tissue injury.

The best way to avoid injury and increase flexibility is to have your players, especially your goalies, perform dynamic stretching prior to practices and games. What is dynamic stretching, you ask? Dynamic stretching consists of things like jumping jacks, running in place, arm circles, and standing long jumps. These are, of course, best done before your players start putting their skates on. Another exercise that goalies can do prior to games and practices is to bring a soccer ball and kick it against a wall. This is a great way to have your goalie warm up his legs, reflexes, and eyes.

Goalie Flexibility

Just because you start practice and game preparation with dynamic stretching doesn't mean that there is no room for deep stretching. Deep stretching is best done at the end of the practices and games.

The reasons for the dynamic stretching before the game and the deep stretching afterwards are this: When you do deep stretching, you stretch the muscles so far that they have a greater chance of tearing with the quick explosive movements associated with goaltending. Dynamic stretching, on the other hand, will help your muscles avoid tearing by using explosive movements to loosen up the muscles prior to playing goal.

Performing long, deep stretches after game activity will allow your goalie to stretch the warm already loosened muscles even farther and increase his ability to gain greater flexibility faster.

It is also a good idea for goalies to practice on their flexibility at home on their own time. If they work at home in the mornings or the evenings, your goalies should be able to do the splits in no time, or should I say survive the splits. There is a big difference between just dropping into the splits and ending up in the splits to stop the puck.

Which brings us to the other advantage of flexibility: more saves. Goalies that are flexible can reach more pucks and be in better positions for rebounds. This will cut down on the goals against average quite a bit.

Due to the fact that there is no need to have rink time to have your players work on their stretching, it is a good idea to add 15 minutes of practice time to the schedule: 5 minutes pre-practice for dynamic stretching and 10 minutes at the end of practice for long deep stretching. Make sure players and their parents are aware of the risk of injury without these stretches or they will start to come late or leave early to avoid it.

For more information on stretching, sign up for our biweekly newsletter at www.TheGoalieCoach.com and receive our free guide to the best goalie stretches.

10

Save Techniques

As a coach this is probably the section that you are most interested in reading. You may have even skipped ahead to this chapter thinking the rest of the information is just filler, thinking that the only thing important is the saves. If you skipped ahead to this section sorry to tell you, you will be missing a lot of building blocks to make this part of goaltending possible. I would highly recommend reading the previous chapters to build a solid foundation so your goalie can be the best he can be.

There are a wide variety of saves and techniques that goalies use to stop the puck. In this section I will discuss what the different types of saves are and review some of the proper techniques for goalies to use. However, I want to remind you of this important point. It doesn't matter how pretty or ugly a save is, just as long as it does not go into the net. Even if proper technique is not used and the goalie keeps the puck out of the net, it is a win for the team. The same with goals your players score: Pucks in the net all look the same on the score sheet.

Stick Saves

We will start with the stick. Goalies and coaches often underestimate the power of the goalie stick. It is viewed as useful only for playing the puck or as a last resort, for a desperate lunge for a puck that has snuck past the goalie but not crossed the line.

The stick is useful for both of these things, but the goalie stick is really the <u>first line</u> of defense for a goalie. A little known rule of goaltending (even amongst professional goaltenders), is whenever possible you must have more than one piece of equipment in front of the puck. This goes back to the old Stand-Up goalies as well.

The idea behind the rule is that a goalie cannot control the puck very well with his legs alone. Having the stick down on the rink in front of the goalie's pads allows him to use a solid object to accelerate the puck away from the front of the net and into the corner of the rink. This position of the stick is just as important for Butterfly goalies to keep their five-hole closed.

You should teach your goalie to keep his stick blade at a 90-degree angle to the puck but to move his stick blade in a half circle in front of him, mimicking the crease layout. He should be aggressive to the puck moving his stick out to meet the puck as it comes toward him. This will have a huge impact on the amount of rebounds that goalies give up.

As your goalie gets to more advanced levels of goaltending, he will learn to flick his wrist when the puck hits his stick so that he can basically shoot the puck into the corner of the rink and not have to rely on the momentum from the shooter. Don't push a goalie to learn this too early, however, as the goalie might not be comfortable with it. He might start flicking his stick too early and opening up holes for the puck to go through.

The final note on stick saves is whenever possible they should be backed up by the goalie's pad. If the puck hits the stick funny or the goalie just plain misses with the stick, then the second piece of equipment is there to make the save.

Poke Check

The poke check is a version of a stick save that most goalies use as a desperation move. However the poke check can be extremely useful when the opposing puck carrier gets in too close to the goalie. It is particularly useful when the puck carrier has his head down looking at the puck.

A poke check is executed when the goalie slides his hand to the butt end of the goalie stick and tries to poke or sweep the puck out of the opposing player's stick. If the player has his head down or is otherwise not ready, the goalie can surprise him and knock the puck away. If the other player is ready, he just walks around the goalie and scores. Sometimes the goalie can get lucky when the player panics and shoots too quickly, but it is not something to bet on time and time again.

Save Techniques

This is, however, an advanced move for a goalkeeper. The goalie sells out any chance he has to make a save if he misses with the poke check.

The poke check is best used sparingly to surprise opponents. If a goalie uses it too much, word will spread around the league quickly, and opposing teams will look for easy goals that way.

Kick Saves

Kick saves are when your goalie uses His leg pads to kick out and make a save. Kick saves are somewhat less dramatic than they used to be due to the widespread use of the Butterfly. In the old days with stand-up goalies, kick saves were dramatic kicks to the post. They barely reached the puck with the toe of the skate. Today kick saves still exist, but they are rarely as dramatic.

The usefulness of the Butterfly style means that goalies are on their knees for most of the shots taken against them. Most of the saves that they make if they don't use their sticks properly are technically kick saves with one small difference. Kick saves used to literally kick at the puck to send it back out away from the net. With the Butterfly, goalies are taught to try and move back to cushion the blow of the incoming puck. This way they absorb the force of the puck and they can cover it up.

Neither way is always right or always wrong. In certain situations you will want your goalie to absorb the puck and cover it or kick it out away from the net. Situations when you want the goalie to kick the puck away from the net are usually when the other team has players camping right in front of the net. The goalie will not want to risk stopping it for them to stuff it home. Situations when the goalie should absorb and cover are times when the opponents have sustained pressure or your team is tired and needs a line change.

I like to teach my goalies to be strong with their sticks to help take the guesswork out of which kick save to use. Goalies can always go down trying to absorb the puck if they use their sticks effectively to redirect rebounds into the corners. They won't have to worry about whether they should kick at it or try to absorb it. They just have to try and absorb with their pads and redirect with their sticks at the same time. If they miss with their sticks, then the puck should hit their pads and give them a chance to cover with their glove.

Save Techniques

Stacking the Pads

Stacking the pads is another desperation sellout move like the poke check. Like the poke check, it can also lead to negative outcomes if overused, but in desperate situations there is nothing quite as effective as stacking the pads. Stacking the pads is generally done on breakaways and cross ice one-timers.

To execute this move, kick your lead leg out as far as you can and sweep the back leg underneath pushing your lead leg to a top or stacked position. As the goalie does this, it is important to remember to get the torso and underneath arm down flat on the rink to prevent the puck from sliding underneath them.

This can leave goalies out of position. So teach them when to stack the pads so they do not overuse it.

Glove & Blocker Saves

Glove and blocker saves give the goalie the best chance at getting a much needed stoppage in play. They are also the goalies best weapon for limiting rebounds.

The idea behind the glove save is very simple; but as simple as it is, nothing can be more electrifying or momentum changing as a good glove save.

To properly execute a glove save, the goalie needs to think of his glove as being his third eye. A goalie cannot make a save with the glove if that eye is not open at all times. Have your goalie practice keeping that glove/eye open when in his stance at all times. Other than that, like much of goaltending it is simple hand/eye coordination.

The other main use a goalie has for his glove is to cover the puck when it is near his crease. It is the best and safest way to get a stoppage in play. The opposing team will try and dig it out, but the referee should blow the whistle quickly.

One last quick thought about glove saves before moving on. A goalie should not make a practice of reaching across his body to try and catch the puck backhanded. Only in last-chance desperation mode is this okay. When it comes to the glove and blocker, the goalie should think of his body in halves. Each piece of equipment should stay on its own half of the body.

Save Techniques

The blocker started out as a protection-only piece of goalie equipment. Goalies had to hold the stick, and that left the back of their hands and forearms exposed to the puck. So they started to make the padding bigger until they developed the modern-day blocker.

The blocker save is a skill that a lot of young goalies neglect. It's not always their fault as the shooters like to shoot high glove to prove how good they are. The blocker, like the stick, is best used to redirect pucks into the corner or out of play. If possible, the goalie should always angle his blockers to keep the puck from harm's way.

Upper Body Saves

In other reference books the upper body or chest save is not generally discussed much. However it is one of the most valuable things you can teach your goalie. If your goalie has followed and practiced all of the teachings in this book, your goalie will be in the correct position at the right time and have a lot of pucks shot directly into his chest.

If your goalie does not learn about chest saves, then most of the time the puck will bounce off of him right in front for a bad rebound. To combat this you need to teach your goalie how to scrunch up, if you will, and absorb the force of the puck. Goalies that do this well rarely ever leave rebounds. This is often the difference between great goalies and poor goalies at the NHL level. Great goalies are always in position and leave few rebounds. Bad goalies leave rebounds all over the rink.

To teach your goalies how to make proper chest saves, make sure they keep their upper bodies as big and imposing as possible until the puck is shot. Then once they see the puck heading towards their upper bodies, they try and crunch their stomachs as tight as they can and roll their shoulders forward. This will give the puck cushion when it hits them, and most of the time it will stick in their chest protectors.

All of the saves discussed in this chapter can be worked on in any drill that involves shooting at the goaltender. To target any specific area have a shooter shoot to the trouble area over and over again. I would highly recommend starting with high shots and moving down to the legs. This way if your goalie is a Butterfly goalie, you can help him to watch the puck instead of just dropping on every shot and trying to adjust to the puck from his knees.

It is a great idea for you as a coach to focus on using proper technique during practice. This will help your goalie not give up as many rebounds during your

Save Techniques

games. But keep in mind that in a game everybody wants to win; don't punish a goalie for finding an unorthodox way to keep a puck from scoring.

11

Playing the Puck

Having goaltenders coming out of their nets to play the puck is a relatively new phenomenon in hockey. For hockey's first century, goalies were told to stay in their crease and not to wander. This all started to change in 1987 when Ron Hextall of the Philadelphia Flyers scored the first real NHL goal by a goaltender.

I say "first real goal" because Billy Smith of the New York Islanders was credited with a goal in 1979. In a game against the Colorado Rockies with the opposing goalie pulled, Smith made a save, and the rebound went into the corner. A Rockies player made a blind pass back to the point. No Rockies player was there, and the puck went all the way down the ice and into the Rockies net. As the last

Playing the Puck

Islanders player to touch the puck, Smith was credited with the goal.

In 1987 when Ron Hextall scored his first goal, it was a different case altogether. The Flyers were playing the Boston Bruins. Late in the game with the goalie pulled, the Bruins dumped the puck into the zone, and Hextall used his skating ability to come out of the net and play the puck. Instead of passing the puck to one of his teammates, he took a shot at the empty net on the other side of the rink. Hextall duplicated this feat two years later in the playoffs making him the first goalie to score a goal in the NHL playoffs.

After Hextall's success, many young goalies started to practice their skating and shooting skills more. Coaches started to notice this, and it has become more and more a part of the hockey landscape. Goalies started to become so good at playing the puck that it was like having a third defenseman on the ice. This hindered the offenses so much that in the 2005 season the NHL introduced a trapezoid behind the net, and goalies were only allowed to play the puck behind the goal line if it was in that trapezoid.

As a coach if you think that having a goalie that can go out and play the puck would be a good asset to your team, then you need to make that a priority. I would recommend following all the steps in the Skating and Mobility chapters of this book.

Aside from having your goalie practice all skating drills with the rest of your team, you will need to have him work on passing and shooting drills. You don't want your goalie to skate out to the puck and not have the ability to move it. Sadly, I have seen this too many times: A goalie skates out and gets the loose puck before the other team and then mishandles it to the other team because he doesn't know how to move it.

I would also recommend that you apply some drills that specifically involve having your goalie come out and play the puck.

One such exercise is the Dump Around.

1. Have a shooter or a coach pick up the puck at the center red line and skate towards the goalie.

2. Before the shooter reaches the blue line, have him dump the puck around the boards.

3. Have the goalie come out of his net and cut the puck off behind the net.

Playing the Puck

4. Have the goalie practice leaving the puck about a foot off the boards so it is easier for a defenseman to pick up.

5. After stopping the puck and leaving it a foot off the boards, the goalie should get back into his net as quickly as possible.

As your goalie gets more comfortable with this drill, add defensemen and have your goalie work on passing them the puck. After he develops comfort with that, add an attacker to the mix so that your goalie can get comfortable with the puck with the other team bearing down on him.

Another exercise that can be incorporated to help a goalie practice playing the puck is to have a puck shot softly into the zone so that it does not carry across the goal line. This helps the goalie learn how to help his team by getting the puck back up to the forwards so they can continue to attack. A more advanced variation of this drill is to add a forechecker to apply pressure to the goalie. This will help with the goalie's decision making, so he will know if he can beat the opposing player to the puck or if he should just stay in the net to make the save.

A great way to incorporate your goalie's playing the puck in a pressure situation is to have them involved in breakouts.

1. Have the players practicing the breakout line up somewhere between their defensive side of the center red line and their blue line.

2. Have a couple of fore-checking attacking players dump the puck into the zone from their side of the center red line.

3. Your goalie should go behind the net to stop the puck and either leave it for a defenseman to start to break out, pass it to a defenseman to start the breakout, or if the fore-checkers are aggressive and the goalie can move the puck to the forwards to start the breakout.

Having a goalie that is a good skater that can come out and play the puck will add a definite asset to your team. It is up to you as the coach; however, to communicate exactly what you want from your goalie. Leaving your net to play the puck can be very scary for a goalie, and it is important for the goalie to know that the coach is behind him. If you are not comfortable with him taking risks by playing the puck, then let him know. If you want him to play the puck, understand that mistakes will happen, and it is

Playing the Puck

important that you do not lose your head if the goalie does make a mistake that results in a goal.

Whether or not you want your goalies to come out and play the puck, you should coach your goalies to be the best they can be. You should incorporate your goalies' playing the puck into practice. It might even win you a few games even if you don't plan it to.

12

Seeing the Puck

For a goalie, seeing the puck is an all-important task. There are two different definitions of seeing the puck when it comes to goaltenders.

1. The act of <u>physically</u> seeing the puck. This consists of situations where your goalie is screened out of the play, and his vision is physically blocked.

2. The act of <u>mentally</u> seeing the puck. This has less to do with if the goalie actually can see the puck when it is shot and more with reading where it is going.

Seeing the Puck

In the first definition the physical act of seeing the puck, it can be very simple to tell if the goalie saw it or not.

You can assume if there is a large crowd in front of the goal that he probably did not see it. Also, if there is a single player on your team or the opposition, the chances of the goalie being screened are relatively high.

Unfortunately, there is not a whole lot to teach goalies about getting rid of the screen. This task usually falls on the defensemen. The best advice I can give you is to teach your defensemen to move the opposing player setting the screen. If they cannot move that player, then they need to front the screen so that they don't make the screen bigger and can block passes in to the opposing player.

Although goalies may not be able to rid the screen themselves, there are a few ways to deal with the screen tactic:

1. Look around the screen. This one is pretty self-explanatory. The goalie stays in his stance and tries to look around the player screening him. The drawback to this is that sometimes you look around the screen to the right and the puck is being shot to the left.

2. Look under the screen. The goalie stays low and tries to keep track of the puck through the player's legs. A lot of times this is done by the goalie going down to one knee with the paddle of the stick flat on the ice. The downside of this is that it limits the goalie's mobility and makes him susceptible to deflections and high shots.

3. Crowd the screen. Most screens take place at the top of the crease. In this method the goalie gets right out on the screen so that the goalie's body is touching the screener's body. This can be effective because depending on the size of the screener versus the goalie, the goalie can see over the screener's shoulder to the shooter. This can also make the screener uncomfortable. He is not allowed to interfere with the goaltender so he has to walk a fine line when moving to not get a penalty. The third reason for this technique is in case of deflections. The shorter the distance between the deflection and the goalie the greater chance of making the save. The drawback to this technique is that sometimes your defensemen will knock opposing players down on top of your goalie.

Seeing the Puck

The second definition of seeing the puck emphasizes more of a mental thing and, therefore, has a lot more gray area for interpretation.

It is hard for people who have never played goalie to understand this concept. When you are not seeing the puck, mentally you still see the puck. You see the puck when it is passed around the rink. When you stop seeing the puck is when it is shot. A goaltender that is on top of his game will see the puck come off of the stick of an opponent. He will see the revolutions the puck makes as it travels through the air. He will know where it is going the instant it is shot at him.

Goalies that are not seeing the puck will not see any of the above. Goalies that are not seeing the puck will see a blur. Most goalies will disguise the fact that they are not seeing the puck with the use of strong angle play and the Butterfly. They will drop to their knees with every shot. This takes away the lower half of the net so they will make saves on most low shots even though they won't actually know where the puck is going.

Here are some ways to tell if a goalie is seeing the puck:

- When a goalie is seeing the puck, he does not drop to his knees when a puck is shot high and wide.

- When a goalie is seeing the puck you can notice his head following the flight of the puck.

- When a goalie is seeing the puck, he controls more rebound.

- When a goalie is seeing the puck, he helps direct the defensive players more.

- When a goalie is seeing the puck, he plays with more confidence, which you will find is one of the most important parts of goaltending.

Goalies that are in slumps are the most likely culprits to not see the puck. Sometimes it is just something they need to work through. This is why learning angles it so important. It allows a bit more leeway and doesn't hurt the team as much to let the goalies work through it. For more tips on how to improve your goalie's ability to see the puck, read the chapter on Focus or visit the forums at www.TheGoalieCoach.com.

13

Fear of the Puck

For goalies starting out, especially young goalies', being afraid of the puck is a very natural thing. Human instinct is to avoid things coming directly at us. It takes a lot of patience and training to remove this natural reaction from our bodies.

For whatever reason, humans tend to flinch and turn their backs towards whatever is coming at them. I don't know if instinctually we feel that our backs can take more punishment that it won't hurt as much or if it is purely based on the sight of something coming at us. No matter the reason for it, it is the worst thing a goalie can do.

The Goalie Coach Handbook

Goalies wear a lot of padding. This is part of the attraction to the position for young and inexperienced players. The one thing most people don't realize about the goalie's padding is that it is all in the front. There is very little padding on the back side of goaltenders. So when your goalies follow their natural instincts and turn their backs to the puck, they expose the unprotected sides and backs of their bodies. Needless to say that if this happens to a goalie, and he is hit by a puck in the process, then easing his fear of the puck becomes much harder.

Aside from the obvious reason of not exposing the unprotected part of their bodies to the puck, keeping your goalies facing forward has another benefit. Goalies that are focusing on what is coming at them can protect their minds from the fear of the unknown. When a goalie can see the puck and knows where it is going and what it is going to hit, then there is nothing to be afraid of.

Here is a quick example: Have you ever watched an NHL game when a puck is shot into the player's bench? Every player and coach in the bench area usually flinches, even the backup goalie. Now, it is understandable for the coaches and even some of the players to flinch, but the backup goalie? The backup makes a living stopping the puck. Why

Fear of the Puck

would he flinch? I believe it is because the goalie is not focusing on the puck. I have seen backups that are paying attention to the play calmly and casually reach out and catch the puck as it goes into the bench area, and I have seen the same goalies dive under the boards like the other players and coaches.

Keep in mind that your goalies need to keep the front of their bodies square to the puck and keep focus so that they know where the puck is going. The only way to overcome fear of the unknown is to make it known. A goalie will have to face shots to realize that as long as he keeps his pads in front of the puck, he will not get hurt, and there is nothing to fear.

You can always try tying your goalie to the posts and have the whole team take shots at him until he is unafraid ala Disney's *The Mighty Ducks*. This could very easily backfire on you, since your goalie may never trust you again. In case you are wondering, it is very hard to coach people that don't trust you.

Speaking of trust, you should be upfront with your goalies. There will be a time when they have to overcome their fear of the puck, and they will become unconcerned with the puck hurting them. When this happens, the puck will still find small holes or creases in their armor, and it will hurt. The best way to avoid this is to maintain a high level of focus. This will keep them safer, and they will stop more pucks.

14

Focus

The difference between a goalie that can focus and one that can't is huge. Goalies that can focus have tremendous upside even before they learn all of the ins and outs of goaltending.

Focus is closely related to fear of the puck and seeing the puck. Goalies that can commit to focus can overcome their fears by knowing where the puck is going. This is also tremendously helpful in stopping the puck. Goalies that are focused can see the puck better and will make more saves on rebounds than goalies that are not.

Focus is something that comes naturally to some goalies, but many others have to work at it. If your goalie seems to lack focus, there is no reason for you to worry. Contrary to popular belief, goalies can be trained to focus. It takes lots of practice and patience, but it can be done.

The nice thing about improving one's focus is that while you do need to practice focus on the rink during practice, you can also assign it as homework for a goalie to work on.

First let us talk about what you can do for your goalies at the rink. If it is not important enough for you to work on during practice, then your goalie will not think it is important enough to work on at home.

To help your goalies practice on their focus at the rink, you need to incorporate screens into their drills. This will help your skaters too, as it will help them time when to screen the goalies you will be facing on offense.

One drill for you to run is called the Timed Screen.

1. Place all of your practice pucks just inside the blue line on one side of the rink. Have half of your players form a shooting line there.

2. Have the other half line up at the offensive zone half-boards on the opposite side of the rink.

Focus

3. Have your goalie get set to face the face shots from the shooting line.

4. On your whistle have one skater from the half-boards skate towards the front of the net and cross in front of the goalie's line of sight.

5. Instruct the shooters in the line that they are to try and time a shot from the point so that it reaches the goalie as the skater from the half-boards crosses in front of him.

6. Once the shot has been taken, have the shooter move to the end of the screen line and the skater move to the end of the shooting line.

7. Make sure each player gets at least two chances to do each, so that they understand the importance.

When running this drill, do not allow the skaters from the half-boards to stop in front of the goalie. This drill is about two things, the goalie's ability to focus on the puck with traffic in front of the net and teaching your shooters how to use moving screens.

Another exercise you can use to help your goalies work on their focus in practice is to assign a pest. A pest is someone that will stand next to the goalie and use a stick to tap his pads in different places to try and draw his attention while he is facing shots. Sometimes it is beneficial to do this task yourself or have an assistant coach do it at first so that your players understand how and when to do it.

As for the homework you can assign to goalies, this can be anything you can think of that will help a goalie increase his focus. He can watch NHL games on TV and practice on following the puck instead of the play. This will also help him to focus on the puck and read the play at the same time. Playing certain video games can help with focus, too. It might be a good idea for you to talk with your goalie's parents before you assign this type of focus homework. If need be, www.TheGoalieCoach.com can create a homework regimen to tie to the specific needs of your team. You can also tell your goalies that they can play board games that test tactive focus such as Operation or fast-paced card games that test speed focus such as Out.

There are also other less exciting exercises that goalies can do. For example, when I wanted to work on my focus, I would go out to a busy street by my house, sit on one side, and pick a spot on a building

Focus

on the opposite side. I would time how long I could look at that spot through the passing traffic. After I finished, I would try to beat my time. As I said, this is not the most exciting of exercises, but it worked.

There are many other ways to help your goalies enhance their focus. It is really about creativity. You can come up with your own ways or collaborate with their parents. Just remember before you come up with new things, to think them through thoroughly. You don't want to just throw exercises at your goalies that don't achieve the intended purpose. For more information on focus, log on to the forums at www.TheGoalieoCoach.com.

15

Pulling Your Goalie

Sometimes in hockey it will be necessary to pull your goalie from the game in the middle of the game. This can be done for a couple of reasons, and it is purely the coach's decision to make. You must keep in mind, though, that this can be a very delicate and damaging situation for a goalkeeper. Here are some of the reasons that you as a coach might want to pull your goalie and some insights to the goalies' thoughts that are being pulled.

Situation #1

The goalie lets in several soft goals. Some nights players just don't have it all going on. Goalies are the same way. Sometimes no matter what a goalie does the puck will find a way into the net.

Pulling Your Goalie

In this situation most goalies will understand being pulled from the game. They may not like it, but goalies know when they let in easy goals and they will understand. In fact, there are times when a goalie is not playing well and the coach leaves them in the game that they get mad at the coaches for leaving them out there.

Situation #2

Another situation that as a coach you might pull your goalie from the game is that the team is playing poorly and the goalie is getting shelled with goals. This will happen from time to time as well. The goalie himself may not be playing poorly, but the team in front of him is. If this is the case, pulling your goalie can help on two levels. One is: It will save your goalie for future games, both in energy and the all-important confidence. Goalies, even very good ones, can suffer from a lack of confidence if they get shelled in a game, even if they received no help from their team. The other way pulling your goalie in this situation can pay off is that it can send a wake-up call to the rest of your team. If they know the goalie is not playing as badly as the scoreboard indicates he is, they will often pick up their own playing level to try and help the goalie save face.

In this situation, the goalie will usually take it one of two ways. The goalie can understand and welcome the rest, or the goalie can be upset that he is spending the rest of the game on the bench. Personally, unless the goalie has played a lot of games in a row and is dead tired, I would prefer my goalies to be upset when pulled in this situation. I think a goalie's competitive spirit should be challenged by a game like this. He should want to be out there to keep his team in the game.

Situation #3

The last reason that coaches have been known to pull their goalies is the coach thinks that public humiliation will motivate the goalie. This rarely works. It is up to you as a coach to decide if you have one of the rare cases that responds to this. Most of the time, however, it will result in a loss of confidence for even a strong-minded goalie; and a goalie with less confidence will not help the team at all.

The most famous example of how handling a goalie this way can backfire is the case of Patrick Roy and the Montreal Canadiens. In 1995 arguably the greatest goalie in NHL history played the worst game of his life. Roy allowed five goals on 17 shots in the

Pulling Your Goalie

first period. Rather than pulling his goalie to start the second period the coach put Roy back out on the ice to humble him. Roy was finally pulled in the second period after allowing a total of nine goals on 26 shots. When he was finally pulled Roy bypassed the coach and told the team president who was sitting in the stands behind the bench "it's my last game in Montreal". Four days later Roy was traded to the Colorado Avalanche, who behind Roy's solid goaltending won the Stanley Cup that season and became a perennial power for the rest of Roy's career. At the time of this writing the Canadiens have never fully recovered from game.

As a coach, you have to be careful not to pull your goalie too many times in any of these situations. If every time your team defense is not up to the task of handling an opponent with a talented offense and your reaction is to pull your goalie, you risk alienating your goaltender and destroying his confidence. Every time your goalie lets in a soft goal or the defense lets him down, he will think he is going to be pulled and will not have his head in the game. He will above all, lose focus.

Keep in mind as you deal with your goalies, especially the young ones, that pulling your goalies during a game can have adverse effects. Make sure that when you do pull your goalie during the game, that it is for the right reasons. Don't be afraid to pull the goalie aside after the game and explain why you did it. If your goalie disagrees with your reasons, try hearing them out. You might find some valuable insight into how he thinks and plays the position.

If you have other suggestions about pulling goalies or dealing with them after they are pulled from a game, please join the forums at www.TheGoalieCoach.com and share with the other coaches.

16

Confidence

Confidence in one's self is important in life. It is especially important for your goalies. Goalies are tested time and time again. Every game every shot on goal is a test for a goalkeeper. While other players on your team can make mistakes and they are covered up and bailed out by their teammates, most of the time a goalie's mistakes end up in the back of the net and on a score card forever.

Confidence is something that goalies cannot do without. A goalie with slow reflexes can easily overcome that by practicing his angles so that he is in good position. The opposite is also true. An athletic goalie can overcome poor angle play to make saves. The one thing that no goalie can hide from is a crisis of confidence.

Confidence is so important that if a goalie lacks the confidence to stop even one player off of the opposing team, it can result in a loss. Here is an example: Your goalie goes out on the rink for warm-ups and happens to notice the other team has a new defenseman that your team has not faced before. Your goalie notices that this defenseman has a very hard shot from the point. Your goalie looks at the rest of the players on the opposing team. Even though he knows several of them are very talented, he is confident he can stop them, but he is not so sure about this new defenseman.

As the game starts, the doubt is in the back of your goalie's head. The game goes on, and your goalie looks like he is in the game making several good and a few great saves against the other team's best players. Next thing you know, this defenseman comes in. You notice that he cannot skate very well; and when he does get the puck, he shoots and it is always to the same spot.

To you as the coach and to the rest of the team, this defenseman poses no problem. To your goalie who does not have total confidence in his ability to stop the opposing player, it is a big problem.

Confidence

Next thing you know, the goalie has given up a soft goal to this player. Then it gets worse: It confirms to your goalie that his fear was right and he can't stop this guy. Now deflating confidence is really in the goalie's head, and he feels that he needs to overplay the opposing player's shot. This opens up the rest of the opposing team to do what they want. Your goalie will start to play his angles off so that he will be in a better position when that defenseman gets the puck. The problem is that the player with the puck had no intention to pass it to the defenseman so he now has a wide open corner to shoot at.

That will result in another goal and another blow to your goalie's confidence. You can see how this can quickly spiral out of control. Not only could you lose the game, but this could lead to a slump and a losing streak.

Seasons lost and playoffs missed can all be because of a goalie's lapse of confidence in himself. One thing you can do to help offset these things is to help instill confidence in the team and the goalie.

Confidence in the team is slightly different than confidence in one's self. Confidence in a goalie's team can be that the forwards will score enough goals to offset bad ones the goalie let in. It can be confidence that the defense will pick up a rebound or an opposing team's player that is open. If goalies have confidence in their team, it can help them with their own confidence.

If a goalie has no confidence in his team, then he must have supreme confidence in himself. This sounds good in theory, but can backfire, since then the goalie will try and do too much, that can get them into trouble. It is best to instill confidence in your goalkeepers and their abilities while teaching your team to play solid positional hockey so that your goalkeepers can have confidence in their team.

To help your goaltenders with confidence, it is important that they know what confidence is for a goaltender. For a goaltender, confidence is knowing

Confidence

that you can stop the puck no matter who is shooting it. Ways to help your goalie's confidence revolve around creating a positive atmosphere at practice and in games.

Ban words such as "can't". Use of these words can be psychologically damaging to people, not just to goalies but to players and coaches as well. To help foster a feeling of unity amongst the team, you should discipline the entire team for using words with negative phrasing. Punishment could include skating laps, suicides, doing push-ups or other calisthenics. It is a good idea to switch up the discipline so that your team will not associate a single exercise as punishment. This could hinder your ability to use this exercise as another teaching aid.

Creating a positive atmosphere will help a lot more than you might think. The mind is a powerful tool and has the ability to make visualizations into reality. Advise your goalies to visualize making saves and your forwards to visualize scoring goals whenever they have downtime. This also helps to overcome the bumps and bruises that come with playing goal. Have your goalie repeat to himself over and over that there is no pain and the mind will help to numb it. You might not believe it, but I swear by it. Since it doesn't cost you anything to try, it's worth a shot.

Remember: There is a fine line between confident and cocky. As the coach you need to make sure your goalie doesn't get too big of a head. Try and have a one-on-one talk with your goalies once a week or so, just to see where their heads are at. If they are having problems, try and help them through it. You should be fine if you create a positive environment for your team. If this does not work, have your goalie join the forums at www.TheGoalieCoach.com to get help from other goalies who might have gone through similar situations.

17

Mental Toughness

Mental toughness is an often overlooked aspect of goaltending that can have a huge impact on how well a goalie plays. This chapter follows the chapter on confidence for a reason. Some goalies will believe that if they go into a game believing they can't lose and they do lose, then taking that approach to the game is wrong. I am sorry to have to say that in hockey, as well as in life, sometimes no matter how much you believe in the outcome you will still lose.

Despite your goalie's best efforts, the opposing team will score goals. Some of those goals will be good goals, goals that no matter what the goalie did will go in. Others will be weak goals that should have never gone in. It is important that as a coach or a parent of young goalies, that you do not overreact to these situations.

The people that will play as goalies for you over the time that you coach are part of a very small group of people. It is important that as a coach you maintain a clear perspective on your area of expertise. Unless you have ever put on goalie pads and played the position of goaltender, there will be things about that position you will never understand.

If you are not one of the few that have put on goalie pads and tried to play the position, then you need to keep in mind that even a goalie that is just beginning in the sport after a handful of games will already have more knowledge than you do about stopping the puck. I know you may not like it, but that is the reality of the situation.

Goalies will know deep down the feeling of what a good save is versus what a lucky save is. They will know a good goal from a bad goal. No matter how black and white it may look from the bench or the stands, it is not always so clear on the rink.

There are many instances that a puck is shot into a goalie's open glove without the goalie ever seeing it. This is not a great save; it is a lucky one. The

Mental Toughness

goaltender will know this, but everyone else at the rink may not.

I have seen a NHL goaltender make a glove save on a breakaway in the playoffs, and heard the color commentator, a NHL Hall of Famer, explaining to the millions of people watching the game what a great save it was and that is why this goalie is one of the best.

The problem is that the commentator never played goalie, and most of the people that were listening to him never played goalie. They all saw that there was a breakaway, and the goalie made a glove save, so it had to be a great save. A NHL Hall of Famer said so.

But if you really watched what happened during the play, you would have noticed that the shooter shot the puck right into the goalie's catching glove. The telltale sign is: When the puck was shot, the goalie's head moved to watch the puck as it traveled toward him. His head watched the puck as it traveled right to his blocker. The problem was that the puck went into his catching glove. The goalie never saw the puck, a lucky save.

Even though most of the goaltender's teammates, the people at the game, and the viewers on TV all believed it was a great save, you can be sure that the goalie knew the whole time that he got very lucky. This is just one example that shows that even a well-respected hockey mind who had been around the sport his whole life could misinterpret a good save and a lucky one.

There is no shame in not really knowing the difference between good saves and lucky ones, Oftentimes the goalie is the only one who really knows if a save was good or lucky. The same can be said about the perception between good goals and bad goals. Sometimes a puck can seem to go right through a goalie, and it is not necessarily a bad goal.

How can that be, you ask? If a shooter is 20 feet from the goaltender and shoots the puck 90 mph to a part of the net the goalie doesn't already have covered like the five-hole, there is no physical way for the goalie to stop the puck.

Believe it or not this chapter is not about how little you know about the goals that are scored on your team. This chapter is about how important it is for a goalie to realize what a good and bad goal is without a coach yelling at him and undermining his confidence.

The best way for you both to understand the differences in goals scored and saves is to talk about

Mental Toughness

it. Don't go overboard because you want your goalie to move on from goals after they are scored and focus on the next shot. A great way to achieve this is to have someone tape the games or practices so that both you and the goalie can review the video and ask what was going through his head. This type of individual review also available at www.TheGoalieCoach.com.

Encourage your goalies to be honest with themselves when analyzing the goals they gave up. This will be easier if they do not feel that they are being blamed. Let them know that they can explain to you what they saw on any given goal. Let them know that even though it may be another player on the team's mistake and that you understand that, it is still not an excuse.

This will help your goalies to build on their mental toughness. They can speak their minds about goals that they do not feel they are responsible for, and you can still reinforce the position all coaches have from an understanding perspective. The position of all coaches should be that as the last line of defense, the goalie is expected to make every save.

Expecting goalies to make every save might be unfair. But if you as a coach don't expect them to make every save, then how are they going to expect to make every save? Mentally tough goalies do believe they can make every save in every situation. Mentally tough goalies play every game as if it is a 0-0 game no matter what the score is. They have the belief that the only shot that is important is the next shot. Most importantly, mentally tough goalies want to face shots late when the game is on the line.

Mental toughness is really just a blend of having the confidence to know you can make the save and the ability to let it go when you don't.

Playing goal is tough enough when you have a supportive understanding coach and can be unbearable when you don't. Try to keep this in mind when evaluating your goalies. Be understanding but firm in your desire for them to succeed and overcome difficulties, and you will be well on your way to developing a confident mentally tough goaltender that can lead your team to victory.

18

The Extra Attacker

There might be one or two total beginners to the game of hockey reading this book. So it will be beneficial to explain in greater detail the concept of "the extra attacker".

In the sport of hockey, the rules don't say you actually have to field a goalie. Your only requirement is to have six players in ice hockey and five players in roller hockey. But before you get too far into that thought, let me say this <u>you will not win without a goalie.</u>

The rules written as they are, however, offer you two golden opportunities to play on select occasions without a goalie in the net.

The Goalie Coach Handbook

1. Delayed penalties: When the opposing team has taken a penalty but the referee has not blown the whistle yet, you can pull your goalie for an extra skater without fear of the other team shooting the puck in. You and your goalie can tell when this is happening because the referee will have his arm raised in the air to signal there is a delayed penalty. If your team has the puck, it is on the opponent, and the goalie can start for the bench. This is a great opportunity because the team that has committed the penalty will have the whistle blown as soon as they control the puck. So the only danger of a goal being scored on your team is if they score on themselves.

2. Losing by a goal or two late in the game: When a team is down by a goal or two late, they will pull their goalie for an extra attacker. It is up to the coach to decide if and when to pull the goalie. Some coaches only do it when down by a goal. Others have done it at three. Some coaches wait until there is only one minute left; while others have done it with six.

The Extra Attacker

As all situations are different, you as the coach will have to decide when and if you are to pull your goalie. It is important that if you are thinking of pulling your goalie, that the goalie knows this is a possibility in your coaching style. As a general rule of thumb, I tell all of the goalies that I coach that if we are losing by two or less with two minutes or under left in the game, then they need to watch the bench for a signal when the puck is out of the defensive zone. If I have other plans, I will usually get word to the goalie by calling my timeout or by having a defenseman relay a message to the goalie at a line change.

The things you need to coach your goalie on to make him ready when he is pulled for an extra skater are simple.

- When the puck leaves the defensive zone, steal a quick look at the referees to see if there is a delayed penalty, especially if they saw something that might have been called.

- When trailing with less than two minutes to go, look to the bench for a signal when the puck is not in the defensive zone.

- When your goalie is given the go-ahead and makes the decision to go, he has to keep his head up. This way he stays in the play. If there is a quick turnover, he can still get back to the net.

- When the goalie is within five feet of the net, the extra skater will be jumping on to join the play. If there is a turnover at this point, it is better if the goalie just comes to the bench. He will never be able to get back in the play as quick as the skater that is jumping on.

Of course, these techniques are worthless if your goalie cannot skate. He will never make it to the bench, and it will be best if you just leave him in the net. This is one of the many reasons to make sure your goalie can skate.

19

Situational Goaltending

To some coaches this might be the most valuable chapter in the book. In this chapter I will explain how your goalie is supposed to handle different situations that arise during games.

Breakaways

A breakaway is when a player on the opposing team gets a chance to go one on one with the goalkeeper. In this situation the goalkeeper needs to move out to cut down the angle. The top of the crease is usually fine, but it is better to come out a couple feet farther if there is room. As the shooter skates in, the goaltender needs to match the shooter's speed. If the goalie backs up too fast, it opens holes in the net for the shot. If he backs up too slowly, the shooter can skate around him and tuck the puck home. A good rule of thumb for a goalie in this situation is: The goalie should be at the top of his crease when the shooter is at the bottom of the face-off circles. This makes it easier for the goalie to cut down angles for a shot and to match speed back to the posts for a deke.

As in all situations, the goalie should concern himself only with the puck's position, and not the shooters position and never ever make the first move.

2 on 0's and 3 on 0's

This is the same as a breakaway, but it involves the threat of a pass. In both of these situations there are multiple opponents attacking the goalie with no defensive help. In this case the goalie needs to be a little less aggressive in cutting down the angles. He should stay at the top of his crease instead of coming out past it. As with the above, the goalie needs to concern himself only with the puck and its movements. He can anticipate a pass, but he cannot move until the puck does. This is a much harder situation for a goalie, but with good mobility and flexibility a goalie can come out on top more times than not.

Situational Goaltending

1 on 1's and 1 on 2's

In this situation the opposing team has one player with the puck coming in against one of your defensemen. Just because there is a defenseman there, the goalie cannot take the situation lightly. Goalies need to be ready for quick shots through the defenseman's legs. They should play their angles properly and not back too far into the net too soon. A goalie should not pay any attention to the battle going on between his defenseman and the opposing forward no matter how close to the net it gets. The goalie should only be concerned with watching the puck. A 1 on 2 is basically the same except you have one more defenseman in the play.

2 on 1's

A 2 on 1 means there are two opposing players for your defenseman and your goalie to deal with. In this case it is your goalie's job to take the shooter and your defenseman's job to take away the passing lane. In fact should be always be considered the rule of thumb. It is always better to give your goalie a clear line of sight to the puck. It doesn't matter how good the opposing player is. Your defenseman should only worry about closing off the passing lane. If your defenseman tries to take the player with the puck, he could end up screening your goalie and allowing a dangerous cross-ice pass.

3 on 1's

Just like in the 2 on 1 scenario, your goalie is supposed to take the shooter. The only difference is that the defenseman needs to choose which pass to cut off. The decision should be based on the opposing player's positions on the rink. The defenseman should take the person without the puck closest to the goalie. This will take away the most dangerous player since he cannot get a pass, and your defenseman should be in position to tie him up so he can't get the rebound.

Rebounds

Rebounds can be avoided if the goalie plays with good technique, but in the heat of the moment this is not always easy. When a goalie is leaving rebounds in a dangerous area, the best thing a goalie can do is locate the puck and try and keep his body as big as possible. If he is down in a Butterfly position, he needs to keep his legs flush with the rink and try and get his head and shoulders high and

Situational Goaltending

squared to the puck. It helps to lean forward toward the puck as this will cut down the angle for any shooters. If the puck is within reach, the goalie should try and cover the puck with his glove and blocker, or it is acceptable to use the stick to try and clear the puck into a corner and out of harm's way.

Wraparounds

When a player tries a wraparound, it is best for the goalie to hug the post and look over his shoulder to find the puck. It is important for a goalie not to panic and sellout in this situation. The best thing for a goalie is to get his lead leg jammed right into the post

with his stick in front of the skate and the post so the puck can't sneak in short side. It is acceptable to trail his back leg low on the ice in case the puck slips through. This gives the goalie options if the shooter doesn't try to wrap the puck in but instead carries it or passes it out in front. If he passes it, the goalie has his leg jammed into the post, and that will give him the power in his planted foot to lunge back across the goalmouth for a spectacular save. If the shooter carries the puck wide and tries to take advantage of the angles, the goalie can quickly move out to cut them down.

In-zone face-offs

When there is a face-off in the goalie's zone, there is something a goalie can look for to tip off what the opponents are trying to do. Look at the opposing center man. If he is on his backhand, he is trying to win the drawback in that direction. If he is on his forehand, he might be trying to win it back, or he might be trying to surprise your goalie with a quick shot or push forward. The goalie should be extra alert when this is the case. Also, have the goalie look at your team's center man. If he is on his backhand and it can be drawn towards the goal, then your goalie must be on alert. Face-offs can be dangerous for goalies that are not paying attention. The way the two centers line up to take the draw can tell a goalie a lot about what those two players are trying to do. As a coach you should always instruct your centers to try and win the draw into the corner on defensive zone face-offs.

Deflections

Deflections are a part of hockey, whether they are intentional or not. A lot of times there is not much a goalie can do in advance to deal with these. The one thing they can do is: If they see a player trying to set up for a deflection, they can move closer to that player. This should only be done if it is safe and they will not be leaving the net wide open. Moving closer to the point of the deflection will help with cutting down the angle and reduce the amount of room the puck has to change direction. After a puck is deflected, it is best for a goalie to aggressively move towards it as a lot of times the puck will flutter and not travel a true course.

Communication

You should coach your goalies to be kings of communication. Goalies will rarely have their back to the play, and they can see things other teammates cannot. You need to encourage your goalies to tell defensemen if someone is chasing them. To call out screens when they can't see the puck. They should call out the shooter and let the defensemen know if there are opposing team players sneaking in behind them. They should call out the puck's position to their players that don't know where it is. When it is late in the game or a power play, they should let their teammates know the time. As a coach you should also encourage your goalie to tell you what they see out on the rink. Goalies have a different view from everyone else. They can tell you what types of offense the opponents are trying to run. They can even tell you how to score on the opposing goalie.

There are many different situations that goalies will find themselves in. In all situations it is important to remember that the goalie's responsibility is the puck. Make sure your goalies understand that fact and stay focused on it. Follow the spirit of this book when coaching your goaltenders, and they will routinely be amongst the tops in your league. If you would like to share your experiences, thoughts, stories, or useful tips to other goaltenders, then please join the goaltenders' or coaches' forums at www.TheGoalieocach.com. Together we can help all goalies take the next step to becoming great players. Better Knowledge equals Better Goalies.

Glossary

Welcome to the glossary, here you will find definitions for some commonly used hockey related terms. For a full hockey photo glossary you can visit www.TheGoalieCoach.com.

The Rink; For ease of understanding there is a diagram of a standard ice hockey rink on the following page.

The diagram calls out the different markings on the rink such as crease, red line, and blue lines. Most standard roller hockey rinks will look similar to this.

The main differences would be that some roller hockey rinks do not have blue lines due to the fact that there is no offside rule or a modified version of offside. If this is the case where you coach assume the blue lines to be much the same position as on an ice hockey rink when explaining to your goalies.

The Goalie Coach Handbook

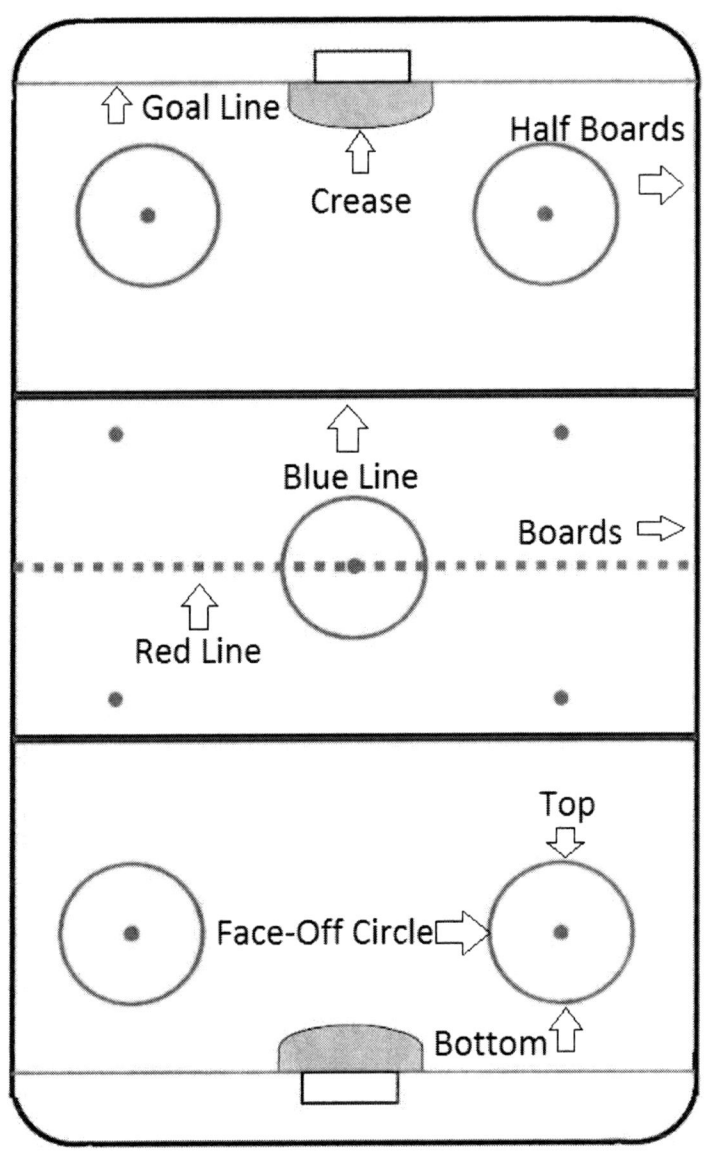

Glossary

- **Breakaway;** When an offensive player has the puck and is in alone on the goalie.

- **Breakouts;** The act of bringing the puck out of your defensive zone to start attacking your opponents

- **Cheat;** To overplay to a certain area of the net so as to be there before the puck gets there. Usually done before the puck is even shot

- **Crease;** The area in front of the net that is the goalies designated safe area. Usually light blue in color it can be different shapes depending on the rink, half circle or rectangular.

- **Cross ice pass;** A cross ice pass is an offensive zone pass that is passed from a player on one side of the rink to a player on the opposite side.

- **Defensive Zone;** See Zones

The Goalie Coach Handbook

- **Deflections;** The art of using your stick to change the path of the puck before it reaches the goalie.

- **Deke;** The act of an offensive player using fakes and stick handling around a goalie rather than shooting the puck past them.

- **Five hole:** The open area between the goaltenders legs.

- **Fronting the screen;** When a player is screening your goaltender your defensive player stands in front of him. To block passes and not create a larger screen.

- **Goals Against Average;** or GAA is determined by how many goals your goalie lets in divided by the standard number of minutes in a game.

- **HECC approved;** The Hockey Equipment Certification Council. HECC certifies hockey equipment for safety.

- **Herbies;** See Suicides.

- **Line change;** Groups of hockey players that are on the rink at the same time is called a

Glossary

Line. Changing these players for new ones is a line change.

- **Neutral Zone;** See Zones

- **Offensive Zone;** See Zones

- **One timers;** The act of shooting a puck directly off of the pass without stopping it first

- **Screens;** Common name for an opposing player trying to position himself in front of the goalie to block his vision of the puck. Screens can also be created by the goalies teammates if not careful

- **Skater;** A forward or defenseman, in this book a non-goaltender.

- **Suicides;** A drill used famously by team USA coach Herb Brooks. Players start at a goal line, on the coaches whistle they sprint from goal line to blue line and back, then goal line to red line and back, then goal line to opposing blue line and back and finally goal line to opposite goal line and back. (also called Herbies)

CPSIA information can be obtained at www.ICGtesting.com
Printed in the USA
LVOW122115020713

341225LV00023B/1223/P